CONQUEROR SERIES

Amanda Musselman

*Early 1900s missionary
to Philadelphia*

ISBN: 978-1-941213-71-1

Cover design and layout: Teresa Sommers

Printed in China

Published by:
TGS International
P.O. Box 355
Berlin, Ohio 44610 USA
Phone: 330-893-4828
Fax: 330-893-2305
www.tgsinternational.com

TGS001040

CONQUEROR SERIES

Amanda Musselman

*Early 1900s missionary
to Philadelphia*

Velina Showalter

Illustrated by Josephine Beachy

Long ago, carriages clattered down the brick streets of
Philadelphia, loaded with fashionable ladies and fine
gentlemen, pulled by prancing horses.
Children played with sticks and hoops under shade trees.

WINES AND WHISKEYS

Shops and markets were full of customers, while in other parts of the city, factories kept workers busy making shoes, watches, clocks, and many other items.

*S*hips were built
in the shipyards
close to the water.

Servants in mansions bustled about to keep their masters happy.

But not all the people in Philadelphia had servants to work for them or money to spend in stores. In some parts of the city, people lived in tall, overcrowded brick houses that were stacked together like books on a shelf. Drunkards loitered along filthy streets, leaving their families at home, hungry and cold.

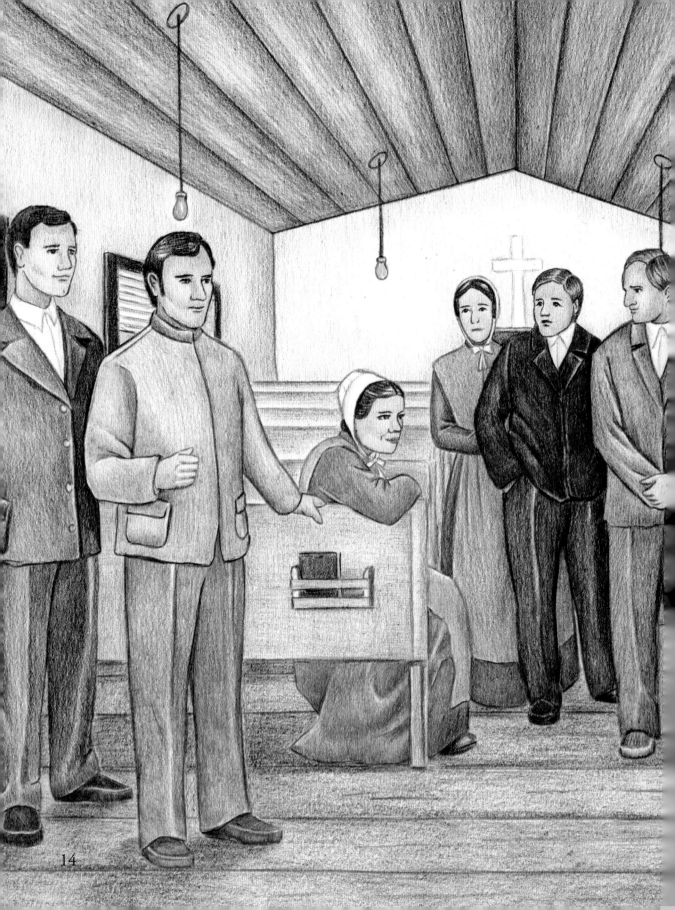

ennonites in Lancaster, Pennsylvania, were concerned about these people. "What can we do to help the people in Philadelphia?" they asked. "How can we show the people in that city the love of Jesus?"

Noah Mack, a Sunday school superintendent, had an idea. "I know a young woman who would qualify to do mission work," he said. "Three years ago during the big blizzard, Amanda Musselman was the only one who came to Sunday school. She walked all by herself across the fields to get here."

Before Amanda became a Christian, she was an energetic girl who loved to go to parties. She swept up her hair and tied it with bright ribbons. She had fake pearls on the collars of her dresses.

After she surrendered her life to Jesus, Amanda wore a head covering of thick white material. Sewn to the covering were wide white ribbons that were tied in a neat bow under her chin. She wore plain, floor-length dresses that included aprons and capes. But more important than her clothes was the joy on her face. She was quiet and kind, and loved serving the Lord.

19

Amanda was willing to serve at the Mennonite Sunday School Mission. She moved to Philadelphia with a friend, Mary Denlinger, in the summer of 1899. The mission instructed them to give comfort where it was needed, visit the sick, and help the poor.

*A*manda's mother was nervous about letting her daughter move to the city. She said, "That city is dangerous, not at all a place for an unmarried girl!" Yet Amanda knew there were many needs to meet, so she began her mission courageously.

First they needed to get a house ready to live in. Amanda was a good housekeeper, and she had plenty of opportunities to use her skills in the house the church rented for them on East York Street. Joseph and Isaac, two young men who came along to help, carried three cartloads of rubbish from the cellar while Amanda and Mary thoroughly cleaned the house. "We have to do something about the bedbugs!" Amanda exclaimed. "I've been bitten too many times. A dose of sulfur should get rid of them!"

23

Besides getting rid of bugs and dirt, the women had to get furniture to use. "What can we use for a table?" wondered Mary.

Amanda had an idea. "Just put this old door on the shelf in this closet and the other end on this barrel," she said.

Since there were only a few windows to let the light in, the apartment was dim. Amanda decided to look on the bright side, though. "All is well," she said. "We have the sunshine of God's love in our souls."

Finally when the house was in order and they had bought some furniture at a secondhand store, the women hung a motto above the door that said, "Jesus Christ of Nazareth, the Holy One, is the head of this house."

*N*ow that they had settled in, Amanda and Mary were ready to invite children to Sunday school. They walked all over the neighborhood to invite the children. Some people opened the door and let them come in, but others slammed the door in their faces. Some places had broken steps and dirty porches.

At one house, they were invited to come in. Stepping inside, they heard the door being locked behind them. When they realized they were trapped in a wicked place, Amanda prayed, asking the Lord to save them from danger. When Mary turned and reached for the doorknob, it opened even though it was locked, and they hurried away.

A neighbor heard what had happened and said, "If you hadn't been dressed modestly as you were, you would never have escaped from that house."

On the second Sunday of June, Amanda and Mary were ready for their first Sunday school class. They decided that Amanda would teach the girls and Mary the boys. Twenty children came that morning. In the evening, nine children came for a children's meeting.

Of all the work they did, Amanda loved working with the children the best. One evening Amanda heard a knock on the door. Three of her Sunday school girls had dropped in to visit her. They cheerfully helped her dry dishes, talking about Jesus as they worked.

"Every sinner we bring to Jesus," explained Amanda, "is a star for our crown."

One little girl said, "I think you will have a lot of stars in your crown, Amanda!"

Although the children were well-behaved and eager to learn in the Sunday school class, boys on the streets tried to distract them.

Ministers had started to come to preach at services for interested adults every other Sunday. One Sunday morning when a visiting minister came to hold a service before Sunday school, Amanda started closing the windows and pulling the blinds before the service began.

"Why do you do that?" the minister wondered.

Amanda said, "Sometimes the older boys stand on the sidewalk and look in the windows and make noises to interrupt the service."

"Put the blinds up and open the windows," the minister said. "I will preach loud enough for them to hear!" And he did.

No noises interrupted the service that morning. A few boys crept up to the windows and listened carefully until the service was dismissed.

Amanda had many things to do besides teaching Sunday school. She started a sewing class for girls so they could make their own clothes if their parents didn't have enough money to buy clothing. She taught the girls how to patch clothes, sew nightgowns, and make tea towels and pillowcases. The mothers were pleased with the work their daughters did.

Amanda and Mary wanted to make a special Thanksgiving dinner for widows and orphans they had met in Philadelphia. They asked for extra supplies from Lancaster, which came to Philadelphia on the steam train. Then they went from door to door, inviting people to the dinner.

It was so much fun opening all the barrels and boxes of food packed with love for this special feast. When everything was spread out, Amanda and Mary realized they had a lot of work to do to prepare the meal. They had seven turkeys, two chickens, a bushel of potatoes, a basket of sweet potatoes, canned corn, canned peas, prunes, cranberries, cabbage, celery, cookies, bread, butter, apple butter, oranges, and pickles.

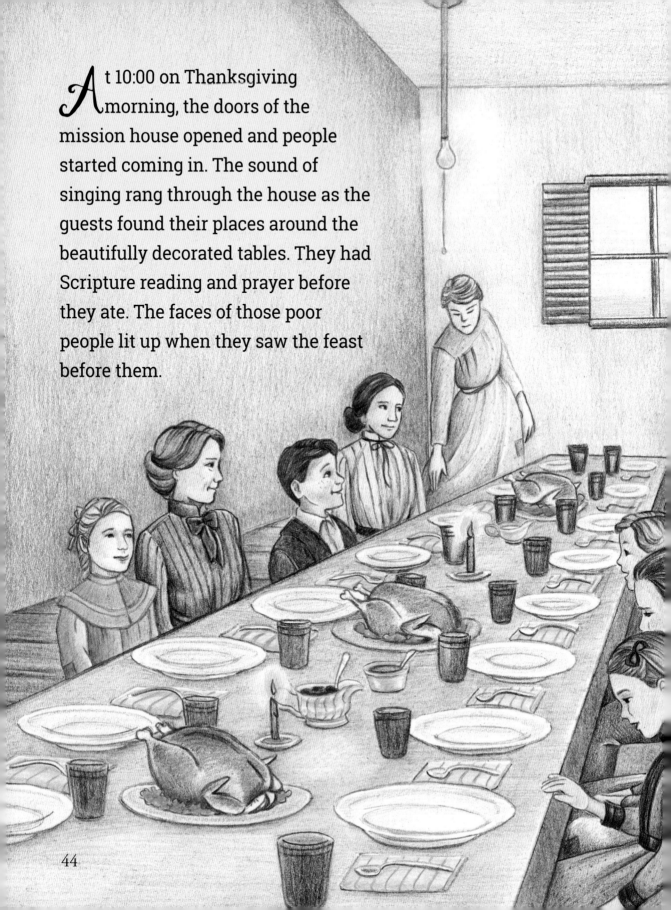

At 10:00 on Thanksgiving morning, the doors of the mission house opened and people started coming in. The sound of singing rang through the house as the guests found their places around the beautifully decorated tables. They had Scripture reading and prayer before they ate. The faces of those poor people lit up when they saw the feast before them.

When they left for home, each guest received an orange and a Gospel tract. Some thanked Amanda and Mary over and over, while others left quietly with their gifts. Amanda hoped that each person had seen the goodness of God.

One day, Amanda heard the doorbell ring. Laying aside her sewing project, she hurried to open the door and welcome the stranger in.

"Hello," he said. "I am a minister from Chester County. I brought you this donation of $38.81 from our congregation."

Amanda's eyes opened wide when she saw the little bag full of notes and silver. "Thank you very kindly for bringing this gift," she said, surprised. "Money is not our main concern, but we need it to keep the mission going. Sometimes we are down to the last potato or cup of flour. But when we pray, a donation comes in the mail or someone knocks on the door and brings us a gift of love."

Money was not the only way people helped with the needs at the mission. Sewing circles sent clothing and bedding. Sunday school literature and hymnals, a new sewing machine, and a new wringer washer were all donated. Amanda wished all the donors could have seen the happy faces of the people when they received the gifts.

Amanda and Mary often gave gifts to the homeless, crippled, and mentally ill people who lived in an almshouse in Philadelphia.

They gave hungry people baskets of food. Mothers who did not have enough covers to keep their children warm thanked Amanda for the blankets she brought.

Happy children skipped home from Sunday school with little booklets to share with the rest of the family. Hymnals were given to people who had no books in their homes.

With extra money, Amanda and Mary bought a brace and some crutches for a woman whose left leg was crippled and her right leg amputated below the knee.

At one house where Amanda and Mary stopped, they found the mother sick in bed. The children were huddled around the table eating dry bread and drinking tea. "Where is your father?" Amanda asked as she placed a basket full of food on the table in front of the hungry children.

Their eyes opened wide as they scrambled around the basket and pulled out a bag of raisins, a string of sausage, a loaf of fresh bread, and some jars of jelly.

"Daddy is out looking for work, but he can't find any," said one little boy.

After Amanda and Mary had cheered up the family and comforted the mother, they walked down the street to another house. There they found Betsy, a fourteen-year-old girl, groaning in pain. She had fallen out of a cherry tree and broken her back. An old lady was taking care of her. Amanda and Mary took time to sing to the helpless girl. After Betsy finally fell asleep, they quietly slipped out.

Their singing cheered many other lonely hearts as well. A doctor who heard their sweet singing said, "Please come to the hospital to sing for the sick."

So one day Amanda and Mary followed a minister as he led them down a dark hall of the hospital. They were surprised to

see about fifty ladies in a large room. They looked so sad and distressed, huddled in their beds. Amanda started singing "Jesus, Lover of My Soul" in her rich, clear voice. Then they sang "Rock of Ages" and other familiar hymns. Some ladies listened attentively, others helped to sing, and some cried.

Amanda and Mary moved on to the children's ward. As they entered, they heard a little boy sob, "I want my mommy!" Amanda patted his back and softly sang a lullaby. She didn't leave until he stopped crying. When they left the hospital, many faces that had been sad were smiling.

As Amanda walked home, she watched the children playing along the streets. She had often wished they could play in the country, so she made arrangements with her friends in Lancaster County to bring some children out to their farm. When the day came, Amanda boarded the steam train in Philadelphia with twenty-four excited boys.

"Be careful," Amanda warned as she helped the boys hop into the wagon that had come to pick them up at the station. "We are going out to the hay field first to watch them load hay with a new machine called a hay loader." Amanda was as excited as the boys as they tumbled into the hay, chased butterflies, guided the horses, ran after the cows and tried to milk them, slopped after the pigs in the mud, picked strawberries, and splashed into the cool

stream to clean up at the end of the day. A tired but happy group chugged into the city that night.

Making other people happy was Amanda's greatest pleasure. For twenty-five years, Amanda served the mission in Philadelphia. Amanda's faithfulness and good example helped many people learn about Jesus.

Facts in Brief

Amanda Musselman: 1869–1940

Parents: Jacob and Mary

Siblings: Jacob, Eli, Amos, Mattie, Anna, and Katie

Baptism:
October 31, 1896, age 27, at Groffdale Mennonite Church

Ministry in Philadelphia:
1899–1924, under the Mennonite Sunday School Mission

Amanda's testimony, written in a letter:
I am happy in the Lord and I am sure He loves me, because He is gently teaching me with light afflictions which work for me a far more exceeding and eternal weight of glory.

Tribute to Amanda, by Mary Denlinger:
Looking back as I knew her, she was never strong physically, yet never wavered from her set purpose of giving Jesus the preeminence in all things. She had the good gift of understanding hearts and the rare gift of giving helpful counsel wisely, interwoven with love. No matter what the hard experiences were, she was deeply rooted and grounded in Jesus and continued to look to Him.

Bibliography

Amanda Musselman Collection (a collection of letters that Amanda wrote to friends and family), archived in the Lancaster Mennonite Historical Society Archives, Lancaster, Pennsylvania.

Ruth, John Landis, *The Earth Is the Lord's: A Narrative History of the Lancaster Mennonite Conference,* Herald Press, Scottdale, Pa., 2001.

Wenger, A. Grace, "Amanda Musselman, 1869–1940," *Pennsylvania Mennonite Heritage,* Vol. V, No. 4, October 1982, pp. 2–18.

About the Author

Velina Showalter was born in 1952 and raised in an Old Order Mennonite group in Ontario, Canada. She taught school for twenty years, the last seven of which were in Farmington, New Mexico. There she married John Showalter, a widower who had five children, in 1989. Three more children were added to the family by this union. After four years in New Mexico, the family moved to Grand Junction, Colorado, where they lived for ten years before moving to their current residence near Greencastle, Pennsylvania. She and her husband are members of the Paradise Mennonite Church in Washington County, Maryland.

Velina loves the Lord and the work of His kingdom. She and her husband actively participate in CAM volunteer relief projects. She also regularly helps at Friendly Village, a church school for special needs children. Writing is not only her hobby, but also a way to bless others. She is the author of *Growing Up with Anna* (a biography of her aunt) and several student workbooks.

Researching to write biographies for the Conqueror Series has given her enjoyable interviews with source persons and rewarding times in historical libraries. Children as well as adults can benefit from Velina's efforts to bring to life outstanding persons in our Anabaptist heritage.

You can contact Velina by writing to her in care of Christian Aid Ministries, P.O. Box 360, Berlin, Ohio 44610.

About the Illustrator

Josephine Beachy lives in central Virginia with her husband of eleven years and two sons, ages ten and eight. She enjoys the quaint charm and history of her hometown, Farmville.

Even as a young girl, Josephine loved to sketch and draw. Now she spends most of her time home-schooling and taking care of her family. Her desire is to continue showing love to those around her.

Christian Aid Ministries

Christian Aid Ministries was founded in 1981 as a nonprofit, tax-exempt 501(c)(3) organization. Its primary purpose is to provide a trustworthy and efficient channel for Amish, Mennonite, and other conservative Anabaptist groups and individuals to minister to physical and spiritual needs around the world. This is in response to the command ". . . do good unto all men, especially unto them who are of the household of faith" (Galatians 6:10).

Each year, CAM supporters provide approximately 15 million pounds of food, clothing, medicines, seeds, Bibles, Bible story books, and other Christian literature for needy people. Most of the aid goes to orphans and Christian families. Supporters' funds also help to clean up and rebuild for natural disaster victims, put up Gospel billboards in the U.S., support several church-planting efforts, operate two medical clinics, and provide resources for needy families to make their own living. CAM's main purposes for providing aid are to help and encourage God's people and bring the Gospel to a lost and dying world.

CAM has staff, warehouses, and distribution networks in Romania, Moldova, Ukraine, Haiti, Nicaragua, Liberia, and Israel. Aside from management, supervisory personnel, and bookkeeping operations, volunteers do most of the work at CAM locations. Each year, volunteers at our warehouses, field bases, Disaster Response Services projects, and other locations donate over 200,000 hours of work.

CAM's ultimate purpose is to glorify God and help enlarge His kingdom. ". . . whatsoever ye do, do all to the glory of God" (1 Corinthians 10:31).

The Way to God and Peace

We live in a world contaminated by sin. Sin is anything that goes against God's holy standards. When we do not follow the guidelines that God our Creator gave us, we are guilty of sin. Sin separates us from God, the source of life.

Since the time when the first man and woman, Adam and Eve, sinned in the Garden of Eden, sin has been universal. The Bible says that we all have "sinned and come short of the glory of God" (Romans 3:23). It also says that the natural consequence for that sin is eternal death, or punishment in an eternal hell: "Then when lust hath conceived, it bringeth forth sin: and sin, when it is finished, bringeth forth death" (James 1:15).

But we do not have to suffer eternal death in hell. God provided forgiveness for our sins through the death of His only Son, Jesus Christ. Because Jesus was perfect and without sin, He could die in our place. "For God so loved the world that he gave his only begotten Son, that whosoever believeth in him should not perish, but have everlasting life" (John 3:16).

A sacrifice is something given to benefit someone else. It costs the giver greatly. Jesus was God's sacrifice. Jesus' death takes away the penalty of sin for everyone who accepts this sacrifice and truly repents of their sins. To repent of sins means to be truly sorry for and turn away from the things we have done that have violated God's standards (Acts 2:38; 3:19).

Jesus died, but He did not remain dead. After three days, God's Spirit miraculously raised Him to life again. God's Spirit does something similar in us. When we receive Jesus as our sacrifice and repent of our sins, our hearts are changed. We become spiritually alive! We develop new desires and attitudes (2 Corinthians 5:17). We begin to make choices that please God (1 John 3:9). If we do fail and commit sins, we can ask God for forgiveness. "If we confess our sins, he is faithful and just to forgive us our sins, and to cleanse us from all unrighteousness" (1 John 1:9).

Once our hearts have been changed, we want to continue growing spiritually. We will be happy to let Jesus be the Master of our lives and will want to become more like Him. To do this, we must meditate on God's Word and commune with God in prayer. We will testify to others of this change by being baptized and sharing the good news of God's victory over sin and death. Fellowship with a faithful group of believers will strengthen our walk with God (1 John 1:7).